Liam Hemsworth

ABDO
Publishing Company

Big Buddy BOOKS
Buddy Bios

by Sarah Tieck

VISIT US AT

www.abdopublishing.com

Published by ABDO Publishing Company, PO Box 398166, Minneapolis, Minnesota 55439.

Printed in the United States of America, North Mankato, Minnesota.
102012
012013

PRINTED ON RECYCLED PAPER

Coordinating Series Editor: Rochelle Baltzer
Contributing Editors: Stephanie Hedlund, Marcia Zappa
Graphic Design: Maria Hosley
Cover Photograph: *AP Photo*: Tammie Arroyo.
Interior Photographs/Illustrations: *AP Photo*: Evan Agostini (p. 7), Suzanne Collins/PR NEWSWIRE (p. 21), Jennifer Graylock (p. 21), John Minchillo (p. 18), Arthur Mola (p. 23), PatrickMcMullan.com via AP Images (p. 19), Chris Pizzello (p. 15), Matt Sayles (pp. 5, 29), Sipa via AP Images (p. 17), Ian West/PA Wire URN:13052280 (Press Association via AP Images) (p. 13), Katy Winn (p. 24); *Getty Images*: Michael Buckner/Getty Images for CFN (p. 27), Ryan Pierse (p. 9), Serge Thomann/WireImage (p. 11); *Shutterstock*: Dmitri Illarionov (p. 8), Andy Z. (p. 12).

Cataloging-in-Publication Data

Tieck, Sarah.
 Liam Hemsworth: star of the Hunger Games / Sarah Tieck.
    p. cm. -- (Big buddy biographies)
  ISBN 978-1-61783-749-4
 1. Hemsworth, Liam, 1990- --Juvenile literature. 2. Actors--Australia--Biography--Juvenile literature. I. Title.
 791.4302/8092--dc22
    [B]
                        2012946488

Contents

Liam plays Gale Hawthorne in The Hunger Games movies. Gale is one of the main characters.

Rising Star

Liam Hemsworth is a talented actor. He has appeared in several hit movies. He is best known for starring in movies based on The Hunger Games book **series**.

Family Ties

Liam Hemsworth was born in Melbourne, Victoria, Australia, on January 13, 1990. Liam's parents are Craig and Leonie Hemsworth. His older brothers are Luke and Chris.

Liam's family is very proud of his success.
Sometimes he and Leonie attend events together.

Liam grew up in Melbourne. His mother was an English teacher. His father worked as a **counselor**. His family was close.

When Liam was about 13, the family moved to Phillip Island. There, he and his brothers spent lots of time at the beach. They learned to surf.

Phillip Island is a popular vacation spot near Melbourne. It is known for surfing and being home to penguins.

Family of Actors

When Liam was young, his older brother Luke worked as an actor. Luke appeared on an Australian television show called *Neighbours*.

Soon, Chris decided to become an actor. Around age 16, Liam became interested too. He started to audition for roles.

Luke (*right*) also started a flooring business. Both Liam and Chris (*left*) worked for Luke while they started out as actors.

A Working Actor

In 2007, Liam got small television **roles**. They were on the Australian shows *Home and Away* and *McLeod's Daughters*.

Soon, Liam got a regular part on *Neighbours*. People noticed his acting talent.

Liam wanted to grow as an actor. So in 2009, he moved to Los Angeles, California. There, he lived with his brother Chris.

In California, Liam and Chris attended events and tried out for many parts. They worked hard to get acting jobs.

Big Break

In 2009, Liam had many movie **auditions**. He and Chris tried out for some of the same parts. When Liam lost out on two important parts, he was disappointed.

Soon, Liam got a **role** in *The Last Song* with pop star Miley Cyrus. Liam and Miley became close friends while working on the movie. *The Last Song* was **released** in 2010. It made Liam well known!

People liked Liam's work as Will Blakelee in *The Last Song*. In 2010, he won a Teen Choice Award for it!

LIAM HEMSWORTH AND GREG KIN

The

Liam starred in *The Hunger Games* with Jennifer Lawrence and Josh Hutcherson. Jennifer played Katniss and Josh was Peeta.

Leading Man

In 2011, Liam was offered one of his most important **roles** yet. He was asked to star as Gale Hawthorne in *The Hunger Games*. *The Hunger Games* was the first of a four-movie **series**. The series is based on popular books. Liam was excited about this opportunity!

In 2011, Liam spent many months in North Carolina during filming for *The Hunger Games*. He learned his character's **lines**. He also had to learn to hunt like his character.

In March 2012, *The Hunger Games* was **released**. Fans of the book **series** were very excited for this movie!

When *The Hunger Games* opened, people attended midnight movie showings.

Liam brought Miley Cyrus to the opening of *The Hunger Games*. They dressed up for a special night.

The Hunger Games

The Hunger Games movies are based on a book **series** by Suzanne Collins. The books tell the story of Katniss Everdeen. Her friends Gale and Peeta help her fight for her life.

Suzanne's books were very successful. The first movie became just as popular. It broke sales records!

Suzanne (*above*) wrote three Hunger Games books, but four movies were planned. The filmmaker wanted to be sure to tell the story well.

THE HUNGER GAMES

New York Times Bestselling Author

SUZANNE COLLINS

An Actor's Life

As an actor, Liam is very busy! He spends time practicing lines and accents. During filming, he works on a movie set for several hours each day.

Sometimes Liam travels to other states or countries to make movies. He may be away from home for several months.

Josh and Liam appeared on a Canadian television show. They talked about *The Hunger Games*.

As an actor, Liam also travels to **promote** movies and meet fans. His fans are very excited to see him! Sometimes they are even more excited to see him with Miley Cyrus or his brother Chris.

Liam has become well known. He appears in magazines. He also talks to reporters on television. And, he and Miley attend events together.

Off the Screen

When Liam has free time, he spends it with his brothers and friends. In 2012, he asked Miley Cyrus to marry him. They are excited to start their life together.

Liam likes to work with groups that help people in need. He has worked with the Australian Childhood Foundation. Sometimes, he attends events that raise money for this group.

Liam and Miley enjoy spending time with each other. Sometimes they go to charity events with other famous people.

Buzz

Liam's opportunities continue to grow. In 2012, he starred in *The Expendables 2*. He also began working on the second movie of The Hunger Games **series**. It is called *The Hunger Games: Catching Fire*.

Fans are excited to see what's next for Liam Hemsworth. Many believe he has a bright **future**!

Reporters often take Liam's picture.

Snapshot

★**Name**: Liam Hemsworth

★**Birthday**: January 13, 1990

★**Birthplace**: Melbourne, Victoria, Australia

★**Appearances**: *Home and Away, McLeod's Daughters, Neighbours, The Last Song, The Hunger Games, The Expendables 2, The Hunger Games: Catching Fire*

Important Words

accent (AK-sehnt) a special way of saying words or phrases shared by people from certain areas or countries.

audition (aw-DIH-shuhn) to give a trial performance showcasing personal talent as a musician, a singer, a dancer, or an actor.

counselor a person who is trained to advise others as a job.

future (FYOO-chuhr) a time that has not yet occurred.

lines the words an actor says in a play, a movie, or a show.

promote to help something become known.

release to make available to the public.

role a part an actor plays.

series a set of similar things or events in order.

set the place where a movie or a television show is recorded.

Web Sites

To learn more about Liam Hemsworth, visit ABDO Publishing Company online. Web sites about Liam Hemsworth are featured on our Book Links page. These links are routinely monitored and updated to provide the most current information available.

www.abdopublishing.com

Index